MINDFULNESS JOURNAL

THIS MINDFULNESS JOURNAL BELONGS TO:

FOR A LITTLE INSPIRATION
follow along at:

@JUNEANDLUCY

@JUNEANDLUCY

WWW.JUNELUCY.COM

Love free goodies? Join our newsletter by emailing us at **freebies@junelucy.com** to receive freebies, discounts and sales info. Let us know which book you bought by putting the book title in the subject line of your email.

Shop our other books at
www.junelucy.com

For questions and customer service, email us at
support@junelucy.com

AN INTRODUCTION TO BEING MINDFUL

Do you know what it means to be mindful? Being mindful means being able to take a quiet moment and listen to our bodies and our minds. Sometimes things happen around us that can make us feel overwhelmed, nervous, tired, or stressed. When we practice being mindful, we are able to take a few deep breaths and remind ourselves that it will be okay.

HOW DO I PRACTICE BEING MINDFUL WITH THIS JOURNAL?

One part of being mindful is focusing on the things that make us happy. Every day, when you start your journal, you will write down three things that you are thankful for. These can be things like family, friends, your favorite food, the show you love to watch, or the beautiful sunshine.

Next, focus on your five senses! When we are mindful, we are able to pay close attention to the world around us and how we feel. So, write down something you recently saw (like a butterfly in the yard), heard (maybe your favorite song on the radio), tasted (like the yummy lunch your mom made you), smelled (your favorite bubble gum soap), or touched (like your dog's soft fur).

Write down how your body is feeling today. Are you energized? Do you have a headache? Are your legs tired after a long soccer practice? And then write down how your mind feels. Are you worried about a big test? Excited for a friend's birthday party?

Finally, close your eyes and take five BIG breaths and write down something about yourself that you like.

TODAY: ___/___/___ S M T W Th F S

FEELINGS

Color in the face that shows how you are feeling

Here are 3 things I am thankful for today:

1.
2.
3.

MY FIVE SENSES

TODAY I:

SAW

HEARD

TASTED

SMELLED

TOUCHED

My body feels:

My mind feels:

CONFIDENCE

Close your eyes, take 5 big breaths, and say "I am awesome!"
Now write something about yourself that you like:

TODAY: ___/___/___ S M T W Th F S

FEELINGS

Color in the face that shows how you are feeling

Here are 3 things I am thankful for today:

1. ....
2. ....
3. ....

MY FIVE SENSES

TODAY I:

SAW ....

HEARD ....

TASTED ....

SMELLED ....

TOUCHED ....

My body feels:

....

....

....

My mind feels:

....

....

....

CONFIDENCE

Close your eyes, take 5 big breaths, and say "I am awesome!"

Now write something about yourself that you like:

....

....

TODAY: ___/___/___ S M T W Th F S

FEELINGS

Color in the face that shows how you are feeling

Here are 3 things I am thankful for today:

1. ....
2. ....
3. ....

MY FIVE SENSES

TODAY I:

SAW ....

HEARD ....

TASTED ....

SMELLED ....

TOUCHED ....

My body feels:

....

My mind feels:

....

CONFIDENCE

Close your eyes, take 5 big breaths, and say "I am awesome!"

Now write something about yourself that you like:

....

TODAY: ___/___/___ S M T W Th F S

FEELINGS

Color in the face that shows how you are feeling

Here are 3 things I am thankful for today:

1. ____
2. ____
3. ____

MY FIVE SENSES

TODAY I:

SAW ____

HEARD ____

TASTED ____

SMELLED ____

TOUCHED ____

My body feels:

____

My mind feels:

____

CONFIDENCE

Close your eyes, take 5 big breaths, and say "I am awesome!"

Now write something about yourself that you like:

____

TODAY: ___/___/___ S M T W Th F S

FEELINGS

Color in the face that shows how you are feeling

Here are 3 things I am thankful for today:

1. ....
2. ....
3. ....

MY FIVE SENSES

TODAY I:

SAW ....

HEARD ....

TASTED ....

SMELLED ....

TOUCHED ....

My body feels:

....
....
....

My mind feels:

....
....
....

CONFIDENCE

Close your eyes, take 5 big breaths, and say "I am awesome!"
Now write something about yourself that you like:

....
....

TODAY: ___/___/___ S M T W Th F S

FEELiNGS

Color in the face that shows how you are feeling

Here are 3 things I am thankful for today:

1. ______
2. ______
3. ______

MY FiVE SENSES

TODAY I:

SAW ______

HEARD ______

TASTED ______

SMELLED ______

TOUCHED ______

My body feels:

______

______

______

My mind feels:

______

______

______

CONFiDENCE

Close your eyes, take 5 big breaths, and say "I am awesome!"
Now write something about yourself that you like:

______

______

TODAY: ____/____/____ S M T W Th F S

FEELINGS

Color in the face that shows how you are feeling

Here are 3 things I am thankful for today:

1. ______________________________
2. ______________________________
3. ______________________________

MY FIVE SENSES

TODAY I:

SAW ______________________________

HEARD ______________________________

TASTED ______________________________

SMELLED ______________________________

TOUCHED ______________________________

My body feels:

____

____

____

My mind feels:

____

____

____

CONFIDENCE

Close your eyes, take 5 big breaths, and say "I am awesome!"

Now write something about yourself that you like:

____

____

TODAY: ____/____/____ S M T W Th F S

FEELINGS

Color in the face that shows how you are feeling

Here are 3 things I am thankful for today:

1.
2.
3.

MY FIVE SENSES

TODAY I:

SAW

HEARD

TASTED

SMELLED

TOUCHED

My body feels:

My mind feels:

CONFIDENCE

Close your eyes, take 5 big breaths, and say "I am awesome!"

Now write something about yourself that you like:

TODAY: ____/____/____ S M T W Th F S

FEELiNGS

Color in the face that shows how you are feeling

Here are 3 things I am thankful for today:

1. ....
2. ....
3. ....

MY FiVE SENSES

TODAY I:

SAW ....

HEARD ....

TASTED ....

SMELLED ....

TOUCHED ....

My body feels:

My mind feels:

CONFiDENCE

Close your eyes, take 5 big breaths, and say "I am awesome!"

Now write something about yourself that you like:

TODAY: ____/____/____ S M T W Th F S

FEELINGS

Color in the face that shows how you are feeling

Here are 3 things I am thankful for today:

1. ____________________
2. ____________________
3. ____________________

MY FIVE SENSES

TODAY I:

SAW ____________________

HEARD ____________________

TASTED ____________________

SMELLED ____________________

TOUCHED ____________________

My body feels:

____

My mind feels:

____

CONFIDENCE

Close your eyes, take 5 big breaths, and say "I am awesome!"
Now write something about yourself that you like:

____

Deep Breaths are Love Notes to Your Body

TODAY: ____/____/____ S M T W Th F S

FEELINGS

Color in the face that shows how you are feeling

Here are 3 things I am thankful for today:

1. ____________________
2. ____________________
3. ____________________

MY FIVE SENSES

TODAY I:

SAW ____________________

HEARD ____________________

TASTED ____________________

SMELLED ____________________

TOUCHED ____________________

My body feels:

____

____

____

My mind feels:

____

____

____

CONFIDENCE

Close your eyes, take 5 big breaths, and say "I am awesome!"

Now write something about yourself that you like:

____

____

TODAY: ____/____/____ S M T W Th F S

FEELINGS

Color in the face that shows how you are feeling

Here are 3 things I am thankful for today:

1. ____________________
2. ____________________
3. ____________________

MY FIVE SENSES

TODAY I:

- SAW ____________________
- HEARD ____________________
- TASTED ____________________
- SMELLED ____________________
- TOUCHED ____________________

My body feels:

____

____

____

My mind feels:

____

____

____

CONFIDENCE

Close your eyes, take 5 big breaths, and say "I am awesome!"

Now write something about yourself that you like:

____

____

TODAY: ____/____/____ S M T W Th F S

FEELINGS

Color in the face that shows how you are feeling

Here are 3 things I am thankful for today:

1. ....
2. ....
3. ....

MY FIVE SENSES

TODAY I:

SAW ....

HEARD ....

TASTED ....

SMELLED ....

TOUCHED ....

My body feels:

My mind feels:

CONFIDENCE

Close your eyes, take 5 big breaths, and say "I am awesome!"

Now write something about yourself that you like:

TODAY: ___/___/___ S M T W Th F S

FEELINGS

Color in the face that shows how you are feeling

Here are 3 things I am thankful for today:

1. ....
2. ....
3. ....

MY FIVE SENSES

TODAY I:

SAW ....

HEARD ....

TASTED ....

SMELLED ....

TOUCHED ....

My body feels:

My mind feels:

CONFIDENCE

Close your eyes, take 5 big breaths, and say "I am awesome!"

Now write something about yourself that you like:

TODAY: ____/____/____ S M T W Th F S

FEELINGS

Color in the face that shows how you are feeling

Here are 3 things I am thankful for today:

1. ______
2. ______
3. ______

MY FIVE SENSES

TODAY I:

SAW ______

HEARD ______

TASTED ______

SMELLED ______

TOUCHED ______

My body feels:

______

My mind feels:

______

CONFIDENCE

Close your eyes, take 5 big breaths, and say "I am awesome!"

Now write something about yourself that you like:

______

TODAY: ____/____/____ S M T W Th F S

FEELINGS

Color in the face that shows how you are feeling

Here are 3 things I am thankful for today:

1. ____________________
2. ____________________
3. ____________________

MY FIVE SENSES

TODAY I:

SAW ____________________

HEARD ____________________

TASTED ____________________

SMELLED ____________________

TOUCHED ____________________

My body feels:

My mind feels:

CONFIDENCE

Close your eyes, take 5 big breaths, and say "I am awesome!"

Now write something about yourself that you like:

TODAY: ____/____/____ S M T W Th F S

FEELINGS

Color in the face that shows how you are feeling

Here are 3 things I am thankful for today:

1. ____________________
2. ____________________
3. ____________________

MY FIVE SENSES

TODAY I:

SAW ____________________

HEARD ____________________

TASTED ____________________

SMELLED ____________________

TOUCHED ____________________

My body feels:

My mind feels:

CONFIDENCE

Close your eyes, take 5 big breaths, and say "I am awesome!"
Now write something about yourself that you like:

TODAY: ____/____/____ S M T W Th F S

FEELINGS

Color in the face that shows how you are feeling

Here are 3 things I am thankful for today:

1. ....
2. ....
3. ....

MY FIVE SENSES

TODAY I:

SAW ....

HEARD ....

TASTED ....

SMELLED ....

TOUCHED ....

My body feels:

....

....

....

My mind feels:

....

....

....

CONFIDENCE

Close your eyes, take 5 big breaths, and say "I am awesome!"

Now write something about yourself that you like:

....

....

Start each day with a grateful heart

TODAY: ____/____/____ S M T W Th F S

FEELINGS

Color in the face that shows how you are feeling

Here are 3 things I am thankful for today:

1. ....
2. ....
3. ....

MY FIVE SENSES

TODAY I:

SAW ....

HEARD ....

TASTED ....

SMELLED ....

TOUCHED ....

My body feels:

....

....

....

My mind feels:

....

....

....

CONFIDENCE

Close your eyes, take 5 big breaths, and say "I am awesome!"

Now write something about yourself that you like:

....

....

TODAY: ____/____/____ S M T W Th F S

FEELINGS

Color in the face that shows how you are feeling

Here are 3 things I am thankful for today:

1. ______
2. ______
3. ______

MY FIVE SENSES

TODAY I:

SAW ______

HEARD ______

TASTED ______

SMELLED ______

TOUCHED ______

My body feels:

______

My mind feels:

______

CONFIDENCE

Close your eyes, take 5 big breaths, and say "I am awesome!"

Now write something about yourself that you like:

______

TODAY: ____/____/____ S M T W Th F S

FEELINGS

Color in the face that shows how you are feeling

Here are 3 things I am thankful for today:

1.
2.
3.

MY FIVE SENSES

TODAY I:

SAW

HEARD

TASTED

SMELLED

TOUCHED

My body feels:

My mind feels:

CONFIDENCE

Close your eyes, take 5 big breaths, and say "I am awesome!"

Now write something about yourself that you like:

TODAY: ____/____/____ S M T W Th F S

FEELINGS

Color in the face that shows how you are feeling

Here are 3 things I am thankful for today:

1. ______________________
2. ______________________
3. ______________________

MY FIVE SENSES

TODAY I:

SAW ______________________

HEARD ______________________

TASTED ______________________

SMELLED ______________________

TOUCHED ______________________

My body feels:

____

My mind feels:

____

CONFIDENCE

Close your eyes, take 5 big breaths, and say "I am awesome!"

Now write something about yourself that you like:

____

TODAY: ____/____/____ S M T W Th F S

FEELINGS

Color in the face that shows how you are feeling

Here are 3 things I am thankful for today:

1. ....
2. ....
3. ....

MY FIVE SENSES

TODAY I:

SAW ....

HEARD ....

TASTED ....

SMELLED ....

TOUCHED ....

My body feels:

My mind feels:

CONFIDENCE

Close your eyes, take 5 big breaths, and say "I am awesome!"

Now write something about yourself that you like:

TODAY: ____/____/____ S M T W Th F S

FEELINGS

Color in the face that shows how you are feeling

Here are 3 things I am thankful for today:

1. ....
2. ....
3. ....

MY FIVE SENSES

TODAY I:

SAW ....

HEARD ....

TASTED ....

SMELLED ....

TOUCHED ....

My body feels:

My mind feels:

CONFIDENCE

Close your eyes, take 5 big breaths, and say "I am awesome!"
Now write something about yourself that you like:

TODAY: ____/____/____ S M T W Th F S

FEELINGS

Color in the face that shows how you are feeling

Here are 3 things I am thankful for today:

1. ____________________
2. ____________________
3. ____________________

MY FIVE SENSES

TODAY I:

- SAW ____________________
- HEARD ____________________
- TASTED ____________________
- SMELLED ____________________
- TOUCHED ____________________

My body feels:

____

My mind feels:

____

CONFIDENCE

Close your eyes, take 5 big breaths, and say "I am awesome!"
Now write something about yourself that you like:

____

TODAY: ____/____/____ S M T W Th F S

FEELINGS

Color in the face that shows how you are feeling

Here are 3 things I am thankful for today:

1. ____________________
2. ____________________
3. ____________________

MY FIVE SENSES

TODAY I:

SAW ____________________

HEARD ____________________

TASTED ____________________

SMELLED ____________________

TOUCHED ____________________

My body feels:

____

____

____

My mind feels:

____

____

____

CONFIDENCE

Close your eyes, take 5 big breaths, and say "I am awesome!"

Now write something about yourself that you like:

____

____

Being mindful is the answer to stress

TODAY: ____/____/____ S M T W Th F S

FEELINGS

Color in the face that shows how you are feeling

Here are 3 things I am thankful for today:

1.
2.
3.

MY FIVE SENSES

TODAY I:

SAW

HEARD

TASTED

SMELLED

TOUCHED

My body feels:

My mind feels:

CONFIDENCE

Close your eyes, take 5 big breaths, and say "I am awesome!"

Now write something about yourself that you like:

TODAY: ____/____/____ S M T W Th F S

FEELINGS

Color in the face that shows how you are feeling

Here are 3 things I am thankful for today:

1. ____________________
2. ____________________
3. ____________________

MY FIVE SENSES

TODAY I:

SAW ____________________

HEARD ____________________

TASTED ____________________

SMELLED ____________________

TOUCHED ____________________

My body feels:

____

____

____

My mind feels:

____

____

____

CONFIDENCE

Close your eyes, take 5 big breaths, and say "I am awesome!"
Now write something about yourself that you like:

____

____

TODAY: ____/____/____ S M T W Th F S

FEELINGS

Color in the face that shows how you are feeling

Here are 3 things I am thankful for today:

1. ____________________
2. ____________________
3. ____________________

MY FIVE SENSES

TODAY I:

- SAW ____________________
- HEARD ____________________
- TASTED ____________________
- SMELLED ____________________
- TOUCHED ____________________

My body feels:

My mind feels:

CONFIDENCE

Close your eyes, take 5 big breaths, and say "I am awesome!"

Now write something about yourself that you like:

TODAY: ___/___/___ S M T W Th F S

FEELINGS

Color in the face that shows how you are feeling

Here are 3 things I am thankful for today:

1. ....
2. ....
3. ....

MY FIVE SENSES

TODAY I:

SAW ....

HEARD ....

TASTED ....

SMELLED ....

TOUCHED ....

My body feels:

....

....

....

My mind feels:

....

....

....

CONFIDENCE

Close your eyes, take 5 big breaths, and say "I am awesome!"

Now write something about yourself that you like:

....

....

TODAY: ____/____/____ S M T W Th F S

FEELINGS

Color in the face that shows how you are feeling

Here are 3 things I am thankful for today:

1. ______
2. ______
3. ______

MY FIVE SENSES

TODAY I:

- SAW ______
- HEARD ______
- TASTED ______
- SMELLED ______
- TOUCHED ______

My body feels:

______

My mind feels:

______

CONFIDENCE

Close your eyes, take 5 big breaths, and say "I am awesome!"
Now write something about yourself that you like:

______

TODAY: ____/____/____ S M T W Th F S

FEELINGS

Color in the face that shows how you are feeling

Here are 3 things I am thankful for today:

1. ____________________
2. ____________________
3. ____________________

MY FIVE SENSES

TODAY I:

SAW ____________________

HEARD ____________________

TASTED ____________________

SMELLED ____________________

TOUCHED ____________________

My body feels:

My mind feels:

CONFIDENCE

Close your eyes, take 5 big breaths, and say "I am awesome!"

Now write something about yourself that you like:

TODAY: ____/____/____ S M T W Th F S

FEELINGS

Color in the face that shows how you are feeling

Here are 3 things I am thankful for today:

1.
2.
3.

MY FIVE SENSES

TODAY I:

SAW

HEARD

TASTED

SMELLED

TOUCHED

My body feels:

My mind feels:

CONFIDENCE

Close your eyes, take 5 big breaths, and say "I am awesome!"

Now write something about yourself that you like:

TODAY: ____/____/____ S M T W Th F S

FEELINGS

Color in the face that shows how you are feeling

Here are 3 things I am thankful for today:

1. ____________________
2. ____________________
3. ____________________

MY FIVE SENSES

TODAY I:

- SAW ____________________
- HEARD ____________________
- TASTED ____________________
- SMELLED ____________________
- TOUCHED ____________________

My body feels:

____

My mind feels:

____

CONFIDENCE

Close your eyes, take 5 big breaths, and say "I am awesome!"

Now write something about yourself that you like:

____

With every breath, I grow calmer

TODAY: ____/____/____ S M T W Th F S

FEELINGS

Color in the face that shows how you are feeling

Here are 3 things I am thankful for today:

1. ....
2. ....
3. ....

MY FIVE SENSES

TODAY I:

SAW ....

HEARD ....

TASTED ....

SMELLED ....

TOUCHED ....

My body feels:

My mind feels:

CONFIDENCE

Close your eyes, take 5 big breaths, and say "I am awesome!"

Now write something about yourself that you like:

TODAY: ____/____/____ S M T W Th F S

FEELINGS

Color in the face that shows how you are feeling

Here are 3 things I am thankful for today:

1. ______________________
2. ______________________
3. ______________________

MY FIVE SENSES

TODAY I:

SAW ______________________

HEARD ______________________

TASTED ______________________

SMELLED ______________________

TOUCHED ______________________

My body feels:

____

____

____

My mind feels:

____

____

____

CONFIDENCE

Close your eyes, take 5 big breaths, and say "I am awesome!"

Now write something about yourself that you like:

____

____

TODAY: ___/___/___ S M T W Th F S

FEELINGS

Color in the face that shows how you are feeling

Here are 3 things I am thankful for today:

1. ______________________
2. ______________________
3. ______________________

MY FIVE SENSES

TODAY I:

SAW ______________________

HEARD ______________________

TASTED ______________________

SMELLED ______________________

TOUCHED ______________________

My body feels:

____

____

____

My mind feels:

____

____

____

CONFIDENCE

Close your eyes, take 5 big breaths, and say "I am awesome!"
Now write something about yourself that you like:

____

____

TODAY: ____/____/____ S M T W Th F S

FEELINGS

Color in the face that shows how you are feeling

Here are 3 things I am thankful for today:

1.
2.
3.

MY FIVE SENSES

TODAY I:

- SAW
- HEARD
- TASTED
- SMELLED
- TOUCHED

My body feels:

My mind feels:

CONFIDENCE

Close your eyes, take 5 big breaths, and say "I am awesome!"

Now write something about yourself that you like:

TODAY: ____/____/____ S M T W Th F S

FEELINGS

Color in the face that shows how you are feeling

Here are 3 things I am thankful for today:

1. ....
2. ....
3. ....

MY FIVE SENSES

TODAY I:

- SAW ....
- HEARD ....
- TASTED ....
- SMELLED ....
- TOUCHED ....

My body feels:

....

My mind feels:

....

CONFIDENCE

Close your eyes, take 5 big breaths, and say "I am awesome!"
Now write something about yourself that you like:

....

TODAY: ____/____/____ S M T W Th F S

FEELINGS

Color in the face that shows how you are feeling

Here are 3 things I am thankful for today:

1. ....

2. ....

3. ....

MY FIVE SENSES

TODAY I:

SAW ....

HEARD ....

TASTED ....

SMELLED ....

TOUCHED ....

My body feels:

....

....

....

My mind feels:

....

....

....

CONFIDENCE

Close your eyes, take 5 big breaths, and say "I am awesome!"

Now write something about yourself that you like:

....

....

TODAY: ____/____/____ S M T W Th F S

FEELINGS

Color in the face that shows how you are feeling

Here are 3 things I am thankful for today:

1. ....

2. ....

3. ....

MY FIVE SENSES

TODAY I:

SAW ....

HEARD ....

TASTED ....

SMELLED ....

TOUCHED ....

My body feels:

My mind feels:

CONFIDENCE

Close your eyes, take 5 big breaths, and say "I am awesome!"

Now write something about yourself that you like:

TODAY: ____/____/____ S M T W Th F S

FEELINGS

Color in the face that shows how you are feeling

Here are 3 things I am thankful for today:

1. ____________________
2. ____________________
3. ____________________

MY FIVE SENSES

TODAY I:

SAW ____________________

HEARD ____________________

TASTED ____________________

SMELLED ____________________

TOUCHED ____________________

My body feels:

____

____

____

My mind feels:

____

____

____

CONFIDENCE

Close your eyes, take 5 big breaths, and say "I am awesome!"

Now write something about yourself that you like:

____

____

There is always something to be thankful for

TODAY: ____/____/____ S M T W Th F S

FEELINGS

Color in the face that shows how you are feeling

Here are 3 things I am thankful for today:

1.
2.
3.

MY FIVE SENSES

TODAY I:

SAW

HEARD

TASTED

SMELLED

TOUCHED

My body feels:

My mind feels:

CONFIDENCE

Close your eyes, take 5 big breaths, and say "I am awesome!"

Now write something about yourself that you like:

TODAY: ____/____/____ S M T W Th F S

FEELINGS

Color in the face that shows how you are feeling

Here are 3 things I am thankful for today:

1. ....
2. ....
3. ....

MY FIVE SENSES

TODAY I:

SAW ....

HEARD ....

TASTED ....

SMELLED ....

TOUCHED ....

My body feels:

....

....

....

My mind feels:

....

....

....

CONFIDENCE

Close your eyes, take 5 big breaths, and say "I am awesome!"
Now write something about yourself that you like:

....

....

TODAY: ____/____/____ S M T W Th F S

FEELINGS

Color in the face that shows how you are feeling

Here are 3 things I am thankful for today:

1. ______________________________
2. ______________________________
3. ______________________________

MY FIVE SENSES

TODAY I:

SAW ______________________________

HEARD ______________________________

TASTED ______________________________

SMELLED ______________________________

TOUCHED ______________________________

My body feels:

____

____

____

My mind feels:

____

____

____

CONFIDENCE

Close your eyes, take 5 big breaths, and say "I am awesome!"

Now write something about yourself that you like:

____

____

TODAY: ____/____/____ S M T W Th F S

FEELINGS

Color in the face that shows how you are feeling

Here are 3 things I am thankful for today:

1. ______________________
2. ______________________
3. ______________________

MY FIVE SENSES

TODAY I:

- SAW ______________________
- HEARD ______________________
- TASTED ______________________
- SMELLED ______________________
- TOUCHED ______________________

My body feels:

____

My mind feels:

____

CONFIDENCE

Close your eyes, take 5 big breaths, and say "I am awesome!"
Now write something about yourself that you like:

____

TODAY: ____/____/____ S M T W Th F S

FEELINGS

Color in the face that shows how you are feeling

Here are 3 things I am thankful for today:

1. ______________________________
2. ______________________________
3. ______________________________

MY FIVE SENSES

TODAY I:

SAW ______________________________

HEARD ______________________________

TASTED ______________________________

SMELLED ______________________________

TOUCHED ______________________________

My body feels:

____

____

____

My mind feels:

____

____

____

CONFIDENCE

Close your eyes, take 5 big breaths, and say "I am awesome!"

Now write something about yourself that you like:

____

____

TODAY: ____/____/____ S M T W Th F S

FEELINGS

Color in the face that shows how you are feeling

Here are 3 things I am thankful for today:

1.
2.
3.

MY FIVE SENSES

TODAY I:

SAW

HEARD

TASTED

SMELLED

TOUCHED

My body feels:

My mind feels:

CONFIDENCE

Close your eyes, take 5 big breaths, and say "I am awesome!"

Now write something about yourself that you like:

TODAY: ____/____/____ S M T W Th F S

FEELINGS

Color in the face that shows how you are feeling

Here are 3 things I am thankful for today:

1. ______
2. ______
3. ______

MY FIVE SENSES

TODAY I:

SAW ______

HEARD ______

TASTED ______

SMELLED ______

TOUCHED ______

My body feels:

______

______

______

My mind feels:

______

______

______

CONFIDENCE

Close your eyes, take 5 big breaths, and say "I am awesome!"
Now write something about yourself that you like:

______

______

TODAY: ____/____/____ S M T W Th F S

FEELINGS

Color in the face that shows how you are feeling

Here are 3 things I am thankful for today:

1. ______
2. ______
3. ______

MY FIVE SENSES

TODAY I:

SAW ______

HEARD ______

TASTED ______

SMELLED ______

TOUCHED ______

My body feels:

______

______

______

My mind feels:

______

______

______

CONFIDENCE

Close your eyes, take 5 big breaths, and say "I am awesome!"

Now write something about yourself that you like:

______

______

Mistakes are proof that you are trying

TODAY: ____/____/____ S M T W Th F S

FEELINGS

Color in the face that shows how you are feeling

Here are 3 things I am thankful for today:

1.
2.
3.

MY FIVE SENSES

TODAY I:

SAW

HEARD

TASTED

SMELLED

TOUCHED

My body feels:

My mind feels:

CONFIDENCE

Close your eyes, take 5 big breaths, and say "I am awesome!"

Now write something about yourself that you like:

TODAY: ____/____/____ S M T W Th F S

FEELINGS

Color in the face that shows how you are feeling

Here are 3 things I am thankful for today:

1. ....
2. ....
3. ....

MY FIVE SENSES

TODAY I:

SAW ....

HEARD ....

TASTED ....

SMELLED ....

TOUCHED ....

My body feels:

My mind feels:

CONFIDENCE

Close your eyes, take 5 big breaths, and say "I am awesome!"

Now write something about yourself that you like:

TODAY: ____/____/____ S M T W Th F S

FEELINGS

Color in the face that shows how you are feeling

Here are 3 things I am thankful for today:

1.
2.
3.

MY FIVE SENSES

TODAY I:

SAW

HEARD

TASTED

SMELLED

TOUCHED

My body feels:

My mind feels:

CONFIDENCE

Close your eyes, take 5 big breaths, and say "I am awesome!"

Now write something about yourself that you like:

TODAY: ___/___/___ S M T W Th F S

FEELINGS

Color in the face that shows how you are feeling

Here are 3 things I am thankful for today:

1. ....
2. ....
3. ....

MY FIVE SENSES

TODAY I:

SAW ....

HEARD ....

TASTED ....

SMELLED ....

TOUCHED ....

My body feels:

....

My mind feels:

....

CONFIDENCE

Close your eyes, take 5 big breaths, and say "I am awesome!"

Now write something about yourself that you like:

....

TODAY: ___/___/___ S M T W Th F S

FEELINGS

Color in the face that shows how you are feeling

Here are 3 things I am thankful for today:

1. ____________
2. ____________
3. ____________

MY FIVE SENSES

TODAY I:

SAW ____________

HEARD ____________

TASTED ____________

SMELLED ____________

TOUCHED ____________

My body feels:

____

____

____

My mind feels:

____

____

____

CONFIDENCE

Close your eyes, take 5 big breaths, and say "I am awesome!"

Now write something about yourself that you like:

____

____

TODAY: ____/____/____ S M T W Th F S

FEELINGS

Color in the face that shows how you are feeling

Here are 3 things I am thankful for today:

1.
2.
3.

MY FIVE SENSES

TODAY I:

SAW

HEARD

TASTED

SMELLED

TOUCHED

My body feels:

My mind feels:

CONFIDENCE

Close your eyes, take 5 big breaths, and say "I am awesome!"

Now write something about yourself that you like:

TODAY: ___/___/___ S M T W Th F S

FEELINGS

Color in the face that shows how you are feeling

Here are 3 things I am thankful for today:

1. ______
2. ______
3. ______

MY FIVE SENSES

TODAY I:

SAW ______

HEARD ______

TASTED ______

SMELLED ______

TOUCHED ______

My body feels:

My mind feels:

CONFIDENCE

Close your eyes, take 5 big breaths, and say "I am awesome!"

Now write something about yourself that you like:

TODAY: ____/____/____ S M T W Th F S

FEELINGS

Color in the face that shows how you are feeling

Here are 3 things I am thankful for today:

1.
2.
3.

MY FIVE SENSES

TODAY I:

SAW

HEARD

TASTED

SMELLED

TOUCHED

My body feels:

My mind feels:

CONFIDENCE

Close your eyes, take 5 big breaths, and say "I am awesome!"

Now write something about yourself that you like:

Kind thoughts. Kind speech. Kind intentions.

TODAY: ___/___/___ S M T W Th F S

FEELINGS

Color in the face that shows how you are feeling

Here are 3 things I am thankful for today:

1. ....
2. ....
3. ....

MY FIVE SENSES

TODAY I:

SAW ....

HEARD ....

TASTED ....

SMELLED ....

TOUCHED ....

My body feels:

My mind feels:

CONFIDENCE

Close your eyes, take 5 big breaths, and say "I am awesome!"
Now write something about yourself that you like:

TODAY: ____/____/____ S M T W Th F S

FEELINGS

Color in the face that shows how you are feeling

Here are 3 things I am thankful for today:

1. ____________________
2. ____________________
3. ____________________

MY FIVE SENSES

TODAY I:

SAW ____________________

HEARD ____________________

TASTED ____________________

SMELLED ____________________

TOUCHED ____________________

My body feels:

____

____

____

My mind feels:

____

____

____

CONFIDENCE

Close your eyes, take 5 big breaths, and say "I am awesome!"

Now write something about yourself that you like:

____

____

TODAY: ____/____/____ S M T W Th F S

FEELINGS

Color in the face that shows how you are feeling

Here are 3 things I am thankful for today:

1.
2.
3.

MY FIVE SENSES

TODAY I:

SAW

HEARD

TASTED

SMELLED

TOUCHED

My body feels:

My mind feels:

CONFIDENCE

Close your eyes, take 5 big breaths, and say "I am awesome!"

Now write something about yourself that you like:

TODAY: ____/____/____ S M T W Th F S

FEELINGS

Color in the face that shows how you are feeling

Here are 3 things I am thankful for today:

1.
2.
3.

MY FIVE SENSES

TODAY I:

- SAW
- HEARD
- TASTED
- SMELLED
- TOUCHED

My body feels:

My mind feels:

CONFIDENCE

Close your eyes, take 5 big breaths, and say "I am awesome!"
Now write something about yourself that you like:

TODAY: ____/____/____ S M T W Th F S

FEELINGS

Color in the face that shows how you are feeling

Here are 3 things I am thankful for today:

1.
2.
3.

MY FIVE SENSES

TODAY I:

SAW

HEARD

TASTED

SMELLED

TOUCHED

My body feels:

My mind feels:

CONFIDENCE

Close your eyes, take 5 big breaths, and say "I am awesome!"

Now write something about yourself that you like:

TODAY: ____/____/____ S M T W Th F S

FEELINGS

Color in the face that shows how you are feeling

Here are 3 things I am thankful for today:

1. ....
2. ....
3. ....

MY FIVE SENSES

TODAY I:

- SAW ....
- HEARD ....
- TASTED ....
- SMELLED ....
- TOUCHED ....

My body feels:

....

My mind feels:

....

CONFIDENCE

Close your eyes, take 5 big breaths, and say "I am awesome!"
Now write something about yourself that you like:

....

TODAY: ____/____/____ S M T W Th F S

FEELINGS

Color in the face that shows how you are feeling

Here are 3 things I am thankful for today:

1. ....
2. ....
3. ....

MY FIVE SENSES

TODAY I:

SAW ....

HEARD ....

TASTED ....

SMELLED ....

TOUCHED ....

My body feels:

My mind feels:

CONFIDENCE

Close your eyes, take 5 big breaths, and say "I am awesome!"

Now write something about yourself that you like:

TODAY: ____/____/____ S M T W Th F S

FEELINGS

Color in the face that shows how you are feeling

Here are 3 things I am thankful for today:

1.
2.
3.

MY FIVE SENSES

TODAY I:

SAW

HEARD

TASTED

SMELLED

TOUCHED

My body feels:

My mind feels:

CONFIDENCE

Close your eyes, take 5 big breaths, and say "I am awesome!"

Now write something about yourself that you like:

Never say, "I can't."
Always say, "I'll try."

TODAY: ____/____/____ S M T W Th F S

FEELINGS

Color in the face that shows how you are feeling

Here are 3 things I am thankful for today:

1. ____________________
2. ____________________
3. ____________________

MY FIVE SENSES

TODAY I:

- SAW ____________________
- HEARD ____________________
- TASTED ____________________
- SMELLED ____________________
- TOUCHED ____________________

My body feels:

____

My mind feels:

____

CONFIDENCE

Close your eyes, take 5 big breaths, and say "I am awesome!"

Now write something about yourself that you like:

____

TODAY: ____/____/____ S M T W Th F S

FEELINGS

Color in the face that shows how you are feeling

Here are 3 things I am thankful for today:

1.
2.
3.

MY FIVE SENSES

TODAY I:

SAW

HEARD

TASTED

SMELLED

TOUCHED

My body feels:

My mind feels:

CONFIDENCE

Close your eyes, take 5 big breaths, and say "I am awesome!"

Now write something about yourself that you like:

TODAY: ____/____/____ S M T W Th F S

FEELINGS

Color in the face that shows how you are feeling

Here are 3 things I am thankful for today:

1. ______________________________
2. ______________________________
3. ______________________________

MY FIVE SENSES

TODAY I:

- SAW ______________________________
- HEARD ______________________________
- TASTED ______________________________
- SMELLED ______________________________
- TOUCHED ______________________________

My body feels:

____

____

____

My mind feels:

____

____

____

CONFIDENCE

Close your eyes, take 5 big breaths, and say "I am awesome!"
Now write something about yourself that you like:

____

____

TODAY: ____/____/____ S M T W Th F S

FEELINGS

Color in the face that shows how you are feeling

Here are 3 things I am thankful for today:

1. ______________________________
2. ______________________________
3. ______________________________

MY FIVE SENSES

TODAY I:

SAW ______________________________

HEARD ______________________________

TASTED ______________________________

SMELLED ______________________________

TOUCHED ______________________________

My body feels:

____

____

____

My mind feels:

____

____

____

CONFIDENCE

Close your eyes, take 5 big breaths, and say "I am awesome!"

Now write something about yourself that you like:

____

____

TODAY: ____/____/____ S M T W Th F S

FEELINGS

Color in the face that shows how you are feeling

Here are 3 things I am thankful for today:

1. ______
2. ______
3. ______

MY FIVE SENSES

TODAY I:

SAW ______

HEARD ______

TASTED ______

SMELLED ______

TOUCHED ______

My body feels:

My mind feels:

CONFIDENCE

Close your eyes, take 5 big breaths, and say "I am awesome!"

Now write something about yourself that you like:

TODAY: ____/____/____ S M T W Th F S

FEELINGS

Color in the face that shows how you are feeling

Here are 3 things I am thankful for today:

1. ....
2. ....
3. ....

MY FIVE SENSES

TODAY I:

SAW ....

HEARD ....

TASTED ....

SMELLED ....

TOUCHED ....

My body feels:

My mind feels:

CONFIDENCE

Close your eyes, take 5 big breaths, and say "I am awesome!"
Now write something about yourself that you like:

TODAY: ___/___/___ S M T W Th F S

FEELINGS

Color in the face that shows how you are feeling

Here are 3 things I am thankful for today:

1. ....
2. ....
3. ....

MY FIVE SENSES

TODAY I:

SAW ....

HEARD ....

TASTED ....

SMELLED ....

TOUCHED ....

My body feels:

....

....

....

My mind feels:

....

....

....

CONFIDENCE

Close your eyes, take 5 big breaths, and say "I am awesome!"

Now write something about yourself that you like:

....

....

TODAY: ____/____/____ S M T W Th F S

FEELINGS

Color in the face that shows how you are feeling

Here are 3 things I am thankful for today:

1. ....
2. ....
3. ....

MY FIVE SENSES

TODAY I:

SAW ....

HEARD ....

TASTED ....

SMELLED ....

TOUCHED ....

My body feels:

....

My mind feels:

....

CONFIDENCE

Close your eyes, take 5 big breaths, and say "I am awesome!"

Now write something about yourself that you like:

....

Today I choose happiness

TODAY: ____/____/____ S M T W Th F S

FEELINGS

Color in the face that shows how you are feeling

Here are 3 things I am thankful for today:

1. ....
2. ....
3. ....

MY FIVE SENSES

TODAY I:

SAW ....

HEARD ....

TASTED ....

SMELLED ....

TOUCHED ....

My body feels:

....

My mind feels:

....

CONFIDENCE

Close your eyes, take 5 big breaths, and say "I am awesome!"
Now write something about yourself that you like:

....

TODAY: ____/____/____ S M T W Th F S

FEELINGS

Color in the face that shows how you are feeling

Here are 3 things I am thankful for today:

1. ....
2. ....
3. ....

MY FIVE SENSES

TODAY I:

SAW ....

HEARD ....

TASTED ....

SMELLED ....

TOUCHED ....

My body feels:

....

....

....

My mind feels:

....

....

....

CONFIDENCE

Close your eyes, take 5 big breaths, and say "I am awesome!"

Now write something about yourself that you like:

....

....

TODAY: ____/____/____ S M T W Th F S

FEELINGS

Color in the face that shows how you are feeling

Here are 3 things I am thankful for today:

1. ....
2. ....
3. ....

MY FIVE SENSES

TODAY I:

SAW ....

HEARD ....

TASTED ....

SMELLED ....

TOUCHED ....

My body feels:

My mind feels:

CONFIDENCE

Close your eyes, take 5 big breaths, and say "I am awesome!"

Now write something about yourself that you like:

TODAY: ____/____/____ S M T W Th F S

FEELINGS

Color in the face that shows how you are feeling

Here are 3 things I am thankful for today:

1. ....
2. ....
3. ....

MY FIVE SENSES

TODAY I:

SAW ....

HEARD ....

TASTED ....

SMELLED ....

TOUCHED ....

My body feels:

My mind feels:

CONFIDENCE

Close your eyes, take 5 big breaths, and say "I am awesome!"

Now write something about yourself that you like:

TODAY: ____/____/____ S M T W Th F S

FEELINGS

Color in the face that shows how you are feeling

Here are 3 things I am thankful for today:

1. ______
2. ______
3. ______

MY FIVE SENSES

TODAY I:

SAW ______

HEARD ______

TASTED ______

SMELLED ______

TOUCHED ______

My body feels:

My mind feels:

CONFIDENCE

Close your eyes, take 5 big breaths, and say "I am awesome!"
Now write something about yourself that you like:

TODAY: ____/____/____ S M T W Th F S

FEELINGS

Color in the face that shows how you are feeling

Here are 3 things I am thankful for today:

1. ______
2. ______
3. ______

MY FIVE SENSES

TODAY I:

SAW ______

HEARD ______

TASTED ______

SMELLED ______

TOUCHED ______

My body feels:

______

My mind feels:

______

CONFIDENCE

Close your eyes, take 5 big breaths, and say "I am awesome!"

Now write something about yourself that you like:

______

TODAY: ____/____/____ S M T W Th F S

FEELINGS

Color in the face that shows how you are feeling

Here are 3 things I am thankful for today:

1. ....
2. ....
3. ....

MY FIVE SENSES

TODAY I:

SAW ....

HEARD ....

TASTED ....

SMELLED ....

TOUCHED ....

My body feels:

My mind feels:

CONFIDENCE

Close your eyes, take 5 big breaths, and say "I am awesome!"

Now write something about yourself that you like:

TODAY: ____/____/____ S M T W Th F S

FEELINGS

Color in the face that shows how you are feeling

Here are 3 things I am thankful for today:

1. ______________________
2. ______________________
3. ______________________

MY FIVE SENSES

TODAY I:

SAW ______________________

HEARD ______________________

TASTED ______________________

SMELLED ______________________

TOUCHED ______________________

My body feels:

____

____

____

My mind feels:

____

____

____

CONFIDENCE

Close your eyes, take 5 big breaths, and say "I am awesome!"
Now write something about yourself that you like:

____

____

Never Stop Dreaming

TODAY: ____/____/____ S M T W Th F S

FEELINGS

Color in the face that shows how you are feeling

Here are 3 things I am thankful for today:

1. ______________________________
2. ______________________________
3. ______________________________

MY FIVE SENSES

TODAY I:

SAW ______________________________

HEARD ______________________________

TASTED ______________________________

SMELLED ______________________________

TOUCHED ______________________________

My body feels:

____

____

____

My mind feels:

____

____

____

CONFIDENCE

Close your eyes, take 5 big breaths, and say "I am awesome!"

Now write something about yourself that you like:

____

____

TODAY: ____/____/____ S M T W Th F S

FEELINGS

Color in the face that shows how you are feeling

Here are 3 things I am thankful for today:

1. ....
2. ....
3. ....

MY FIVE SENSES

TODAY I:

SAW ....

HEARD ....

TASTED ....

SMELLED ....

TOUCHED ....

My body feels:

My mind feels:

CONFIDENCE

Close your eyes, take 5 big breaths, and say "I am awesome!"

Now write something about yourself that you like:

TODAY: ____/____/____ S M T W Th F S

FEELiNGS

Color in the face that shows how you are feeling

Here are 3 things I am thankful for today:

1. ______
2. ______
3. ______

MY FiVE SENSES

TODAY I:

SAW ______

HEARD ______

TASTED ______

SMELLED ______

TOUCHED ______

My body feels:

______

My mind feels:

______

CONFiDENCE

Close your eyes, take 5 big breaths, and say "I am awesome!"

Now write something about yourself that you like:

______

TODAY: ____/____/____ S M T W Th F S

FEELINGS

Color in the face that shows how you are feeling

Here are 3 things I am thankful for today:

1. ....
2. ....
3. ....

MY FIVE SENSES

TODAY I:

SAW ....

HEARD ....

TASTED ....

SMELLED ....

TOUCHED ....

My body feels:

....

....

....

My mind feels:

....

....

....

CONFIDENCE

Close your eyes, take 5 big breaths, and say "I am awesome!"
Now write something about yourself that you like:

....

....

TODAY: ____/____/____ S M T W Th F S

FEELINGS

Color in the face that shows how you are feeling

Here are 3 things I am thankful for today:

1. ______________________
2. ______________________
3. ______________________

MY FIVE SENSES

TODAY I:

SAW ______________________

HEARD ______________________

TASTED ______________________

SMELLED ______________________

TOUCHED ______________________

My body feels:

____

____

____

My mind feels:

____

____

____

CONFIDENCE

Close your eyes, take 5 big breaths, and say "I am awesome!"

Now write something about yourself that you like:

____

____

TODAY: ____/____/____ S M T W Th F S

FEELiNGS

Color in the face that shows how you are feeling

Here are 3 things I am thankful for today:

1. ....
2. ....
3. ....

MY FiVE SENSES

TODAY I:

SAW ....

HEARD ....

TASTED ....

SMELLED ....

TOUCHED ....

My body feels:

....

My mind feels:

....

CONFiDENCE

Close your eyes, take 5 big breaths, and say "I am awesome!"

Now write something about yourself that you like:

....

TODAY: ____/____/____ S M T W Th F S

FEELINGS

Color in the face that shows how you are feeling

Here are 3 things I am thankful for today:

1. ______________________
2. ______________________
3. ______________________

MY FIVE SENSES

TODAY I:

SAW ______________________

HEARD ______________________

TASTED ______________________

SMELLED ______________________

TOUCHED ______________________

My body feels:

____

My mind feels:

____

CONFIDENCE

Close your eyes, take 5 big breaths, and say "I am awesome!"

Now write something about yourself that you like:

____

TODAY: ____/____/____ S M T W Th F S

FEELINGS

Color in the face that shows how you are feeling

Here are 3 things I am thankful for today:

1. ....
2. ....
3. ....

MY FIVE SENSES

TODAY I:

SAW ....

HEARD ....

TASTED ....

SMELLED ....

TOUCHED ....

My body feels:

....

....

....

My mind feels:

....

....

....

CONFIDENCE

Close your eyes, take 5 big breaths, and say "I am awesome!"

Now write something about yourself that you like:

....

....

THANKFULNESS IS THE QUICKEST PATH TO JOY

TODAY: ____/____/____ S M T W Th F S

FEELINGS

Color in the face that shows how you are feeling

Here are 3 things I am thankful for today:

1. ....

2. ....

3. ....

MY FIVE SENSES

TODAY I:

SAW ....

HEARD ....

TASTED ....

SMELLED ....

TOUCHED ....

My body feels:

My mind feels:

CONFIDENCE

Close your eyes, take 5 big breaths, and say "I am awesome!"

Now write something about yourself that you like:

TODAY: ____/____/____ S M T W Th F S

FEELINGS

Color in the face that shows how you are feeling

Here are 3 things I am thankful for today:

1. ....
2. ....
3. ....

MY FIVE SENSES

TODAY I:

- SAW ....
- HEARD ....
- TASTED ....
- SMELLED ....
- TOUCHED ....

My body feels:

....

....

....

My mind feels:

....

....

....

CONFIDENCE

Close your eyes, take 5 big breaths, and say "I am awesome!"
Now write something about yourself that you like:

....

....

TODAY: ___/___/___ S M T W Th F S

FEELINGS

Color in the face that shows how you are feeling

Here are 3 things I am thankful for today:

1. ....
2. ....
3. ....

MY FIVE SENSES

TODAY I:

SAW ....

HEARD ....

TASTED ....

SMELLED ....

TOUCHED ....

My body feels:

My mind feels:

CONFIDENCE

Close your eyes, take 5 big breaths, and say "I am awesome!"

Now write something about yourself that you like:

Manufactured by Amazon.ca
Bolton, ON

20711534R00061